# Route 4, Box 358

AF266861

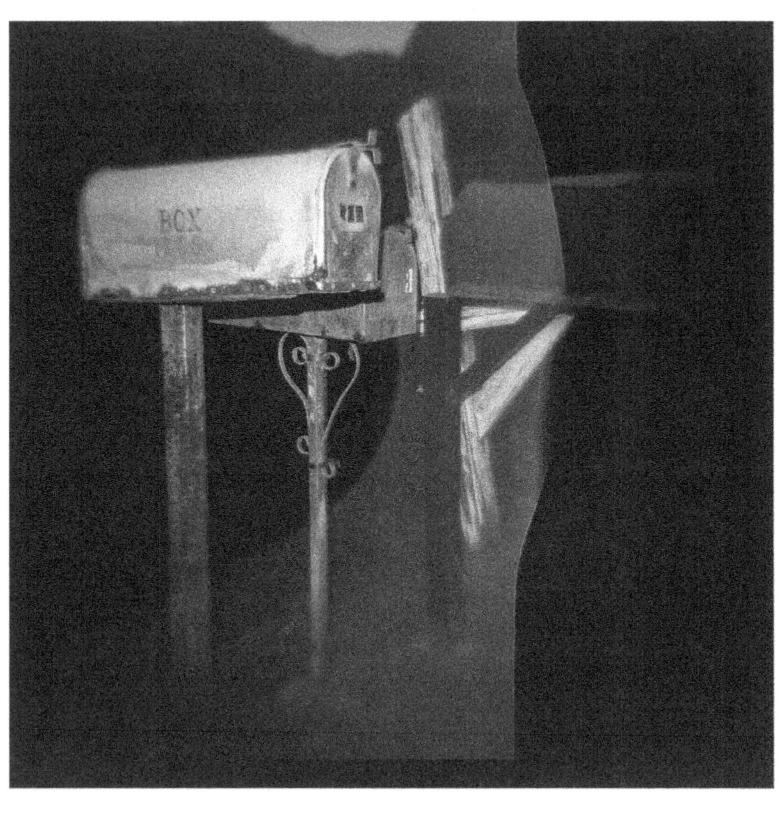
BOX

# Route 4, Box 358

poems by

## Dudgrick Bevins

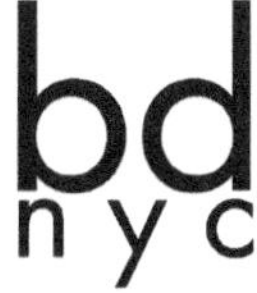

*Route 4, Box 358*

Published by bd-studios.com in New York City, 2018
Copyright © 2018 by Dudgrick Bevins

Photos by Dudgrick Bevins
Foreword by Adam Garnett
Art Direction and Design by luke kurtis

ISBN 978-0-9992078-6-4

Dedicated to blackberries
and everyone who picked them with me
on the roadside.

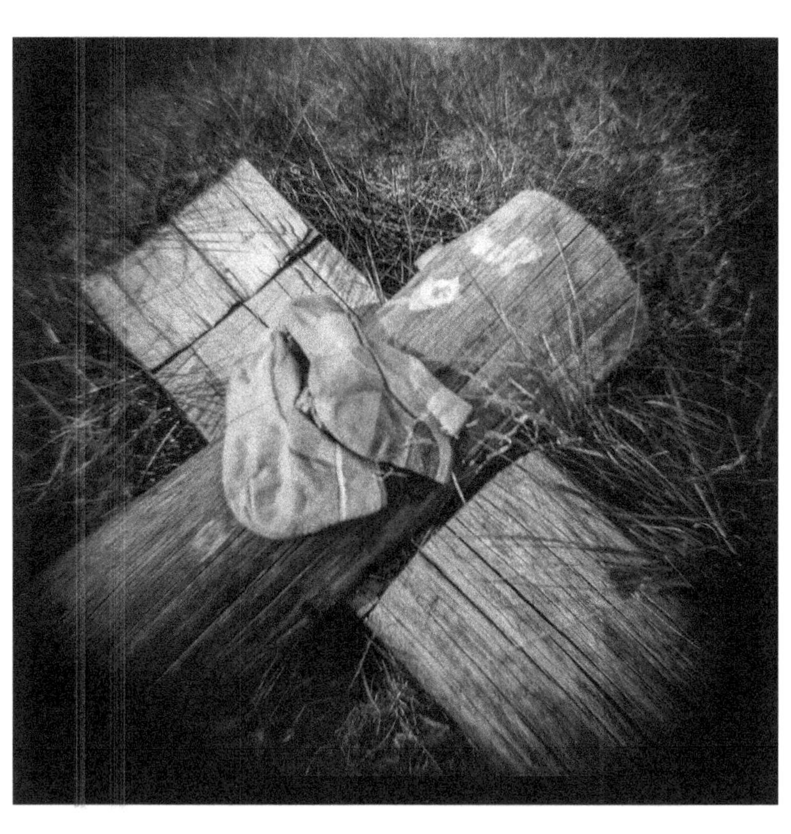

I dwell in a lonely house I know
That vanished many a summer ago,
    And left no trace but the cellar walls,
    And a cellar in which the daylight falls
And the purple-stemmed wild raspberries grow.

—Robert Frost

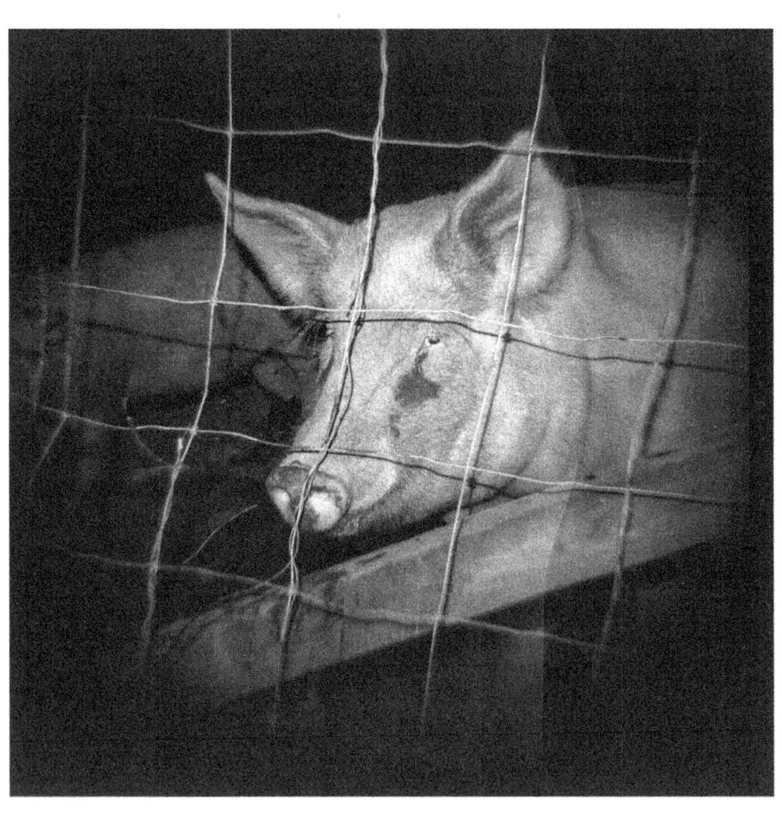

# Contents

## Foreword
## by Adam Garnett

I received a phone call from an old friend I had not spoken with for over twenty years and it sparked my hippocampus – a glass jar of imprisoned fireflies opened inside me. It was as if video footage of my life had been found that had not been seen in quite some time. I was astonished, heartbroken, and thrilled simultaneously to have recovered the black box of such an integral and vintage part of myself through our two-hour-long conversation.

When I read over my colleague and dear friend's first draft of poems that ended up becoming *Route Four, Box 358*, I suffered the same beautiful melancholy and trauma I did upon hearing my old friend's voice on the other end of the line.

This book of poems time travels to a period in America that is suddenly becoming elusive, if not repressed from our collective memories. These poems dig into the soil of a vast subconscious of once common memories shared within the American experience. And even though I did not grow up in the rural Georgia backwoods, this book reaffirms that parallel universes do exist. For the cut of a rose thorn feels similar no matter where planted.

## Author's Preface
## by Dudgrick Bevins

I grew up seventy-something miles from Atlanta in a small town at the head of the Appalachian trail — a town called Ellijay. I grew up among lush green fields where wild daffodils, which we called March flowers, bloomed every spring. I grew up among mountain foothills that looked like children of giants playing under great green sheets. I grew up among kudzu and blackberries and muscadine vines, among fox grapes and foxes and deer and all the creatures that eat wild fruit. It was a beautiful pastoral painting that I called home, and at times I loved it.

I loved the camping trips, the walks in the woods along meandering creeks, and the fresh apple cider I could find at any of the hundred or so local apple houses. What I hated was the isolation from broader culture, the presence of the KKK, and the Bible Belt dedication to various and competing forms of Christianity. I hated what worked to destroy my own difference.

I was a queer kid in all senses of the word and that queerness was undeniable, unavoidable, and unmistakable — though some did try to explain it away as being symptomatic of my artistic inclinations. I imagine people – parents, grandparents, aunts and uncles — saying things like, "Ah, he ain't queer, he's just artsy"; though, I have no evidence this occurred, and when I came out at sixteen everyone took it well, my grandfather commenting when he was told, "I didn't fall off the fuckin' turnip truck yesterday." Acceptance at home or not, my queerness was not popular in school. I cared about the wrong things: reading over religion, animals and art over hunting and booze-hounding. This queerness kept me from investing in the cultural values of complacency, hate, and faith.

This lack of investment encouraged the queer part of me to grow, and the part of me that was

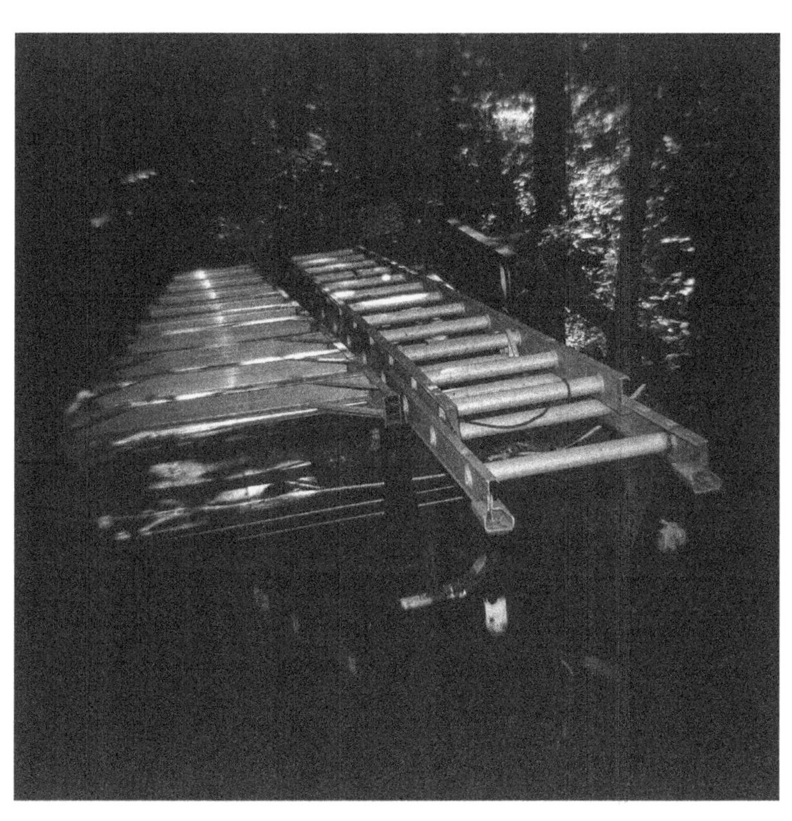

always trying to escape, to see something more, to experience what seemed far away. And eventually I did, but what I found was that distance made me miss my birthplace, to see the beauty I couldn't see while I was in it. Distance gave me the space to process both sides of my experience from all angles, to see things reflected through the prism of age and space. I got to see, for the first time, my home through the eyes of an adult.

In youth, I didn't have the language to express how difficult it is to reconcile a beautiful place with the ugly things it holds. For instance, the majority of the land in my county was untouched national forest bookended with two state parks — a waterfall at one end and Cherokee ruins at the other — and yet this place was the headquarters for the northeast Georgia KKK chapter. They held rallies on the steps of the courthouse. They handed out flyers outside the local Ingles and

Food Lion grocery stores. And at least once they passed their papers up through the windows of school busses. Likewise, when several gay-owned businesses opened in the town, Ellijay became known as Elli*gay*. There was even a rumor that went around about the businesses advertising in Atlanta gay papers, saying, "Come roll in the hay in Ellijay." Mysteriously the gay bed and breakfast burned down soon after. When the businesses moved in I felt more welcome in my hometown than ever before, and when they were assaulted I knew that the message extended to me as well.

I tried, for a time, maybe from eleven to fourteen, to find my place in the religious overgrowth, that kudzu of belief, that overwhelmed not just my hometown but the entire South; however, I found similar contradictions in church: kind, welcoming people who wanted me there but ultimately didn't want either my questioning or my queerness. I found youth pastors who told me to pray on every question, pray on my restlessness, pray on fears. And, I found that prayer did nothing to make me feel more at home in a place of contradictions; I even prayed for three hours straight one night asking "God into my heart" to no avail, and thus concluded that, 1) there either is no God, or 2) there is a God, but a) he doesn't want me or b) God's followers are wrong about the sense of peace that comes with faith. When one of the youth pastors came to check on my absence from church, my father told him I was sleeping, and then once he left told me that the pastor was wearing a Klan belt buckle.

It seems that with time both hate and faith can collapse. Doing research, I found that the northeast chapter of the Klan, the chapter that organized the rallies in town, had disbanded, and now their website was dedicated to the webmaster's collection of "authentic German Third Reich military relics." I like to think everyone got too tired or too educated to be that ignorant, or better yet, that hate was so out of place in such a beautiful landscape.

Living in my own absence of belief, I've found that Amy Hempel's words on art hold true without faith: "Art" she said, is the spiritual nourishment for those "religion has failed." The poetry that follows, I hope, is nourishment for someone other than myself. I hope it serves as food for anyone who knows the tension of living with both beauty and ugliness. I hope it is neither singularly sweet or bitter, but a meal that touches on each part of the palate.

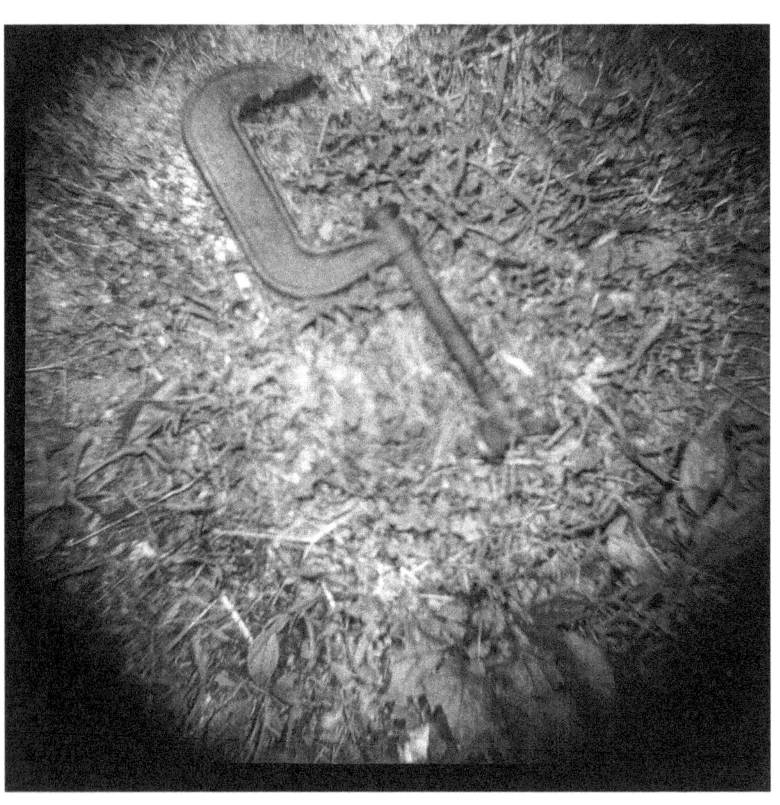

## Rural Route 4, Box 358 I

Kindergarten, an assignment, memorize my address and directions home. Each child had to write them and recite them — a big task for small hands. But I did it. "Route 4, box 358. Turn left out of the school; turn left again and when the road dead ends turn left again, this time on to River Street; go three miles and then left again on to Turnip Town; follow for one mile and left again on Greenfield Lane; when the road forks go right and when it forks again go right again and when it forks again go left one last time." That's how I got home.

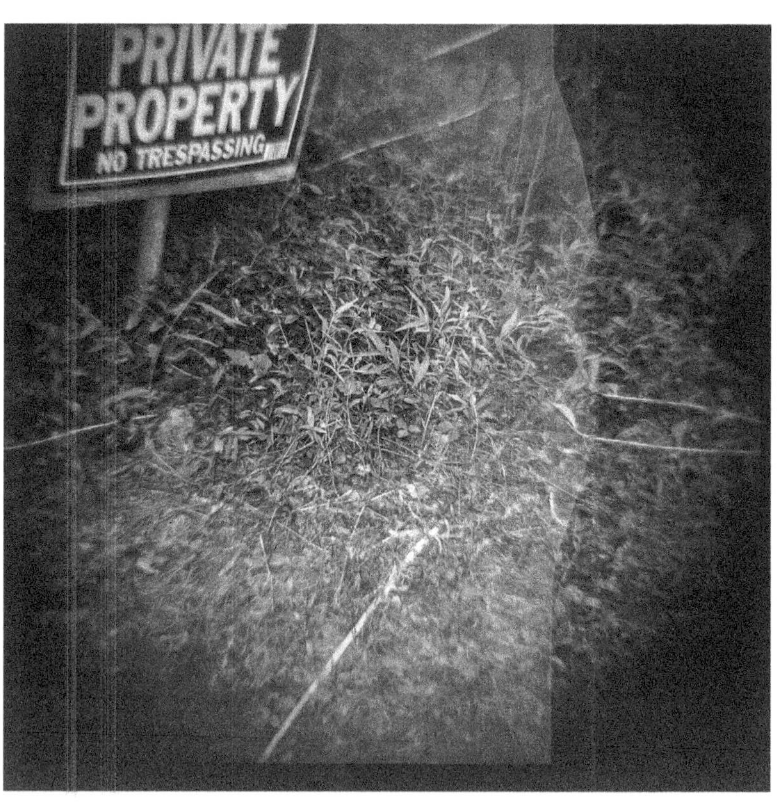

PRIVATE
PROPERTY
NO TRESPASSING

## Klan Encounters Pt. 1


There are still hoods,
Their headquarters
My hometown
With a PO Box
Easily found
With a quick
Internet search.

Sometimes
You can spot them,
Without their cloaks
Without their burning crosses,
Belt buckles signifying
Membership or sympathy.

Look for their insignia —
A red iron cross,
Its points flared —
In Sunday churches
Where men wear jeans
And short sleeves
On their button-ups.

They will be shaking hands
And saying,
"God bless you, now"
And "See you again."

## Reflection: Blackberries

As much blood as blackberry juice went in to those empty butter bowls as we picked our fingers raw between the thorns and thistle. Mosquito laden summer evenings in the chigger briars turned to nights of fireflies and warm fresh cobbler with cool milk. We would have over-picked, but that's impossible; ask the squirrels and crows, annoyed by how we'd eat their food, snacking on the flesh of wild ripe fruit as we'd go. But we had to have enough for winter, frozen into Ziploc bricks, waiting for Thanksgiving or Christmas in the dark recesses of the freezer; or in the case of my grandmother, buried at the bottom of the deep freeze on the porch. How is it we never got snake bit? Maybe our roaming dogs kept us safe as we explored the brambles along the road bank.

**Ghost**

I.

Discomfort plagues me.
Memory
Haunts the same as ghosts.

II.

Nothing is one thing,
No single
Homogeneous goo.

III.

Happiness follows,
Right behind…
There were good times too.

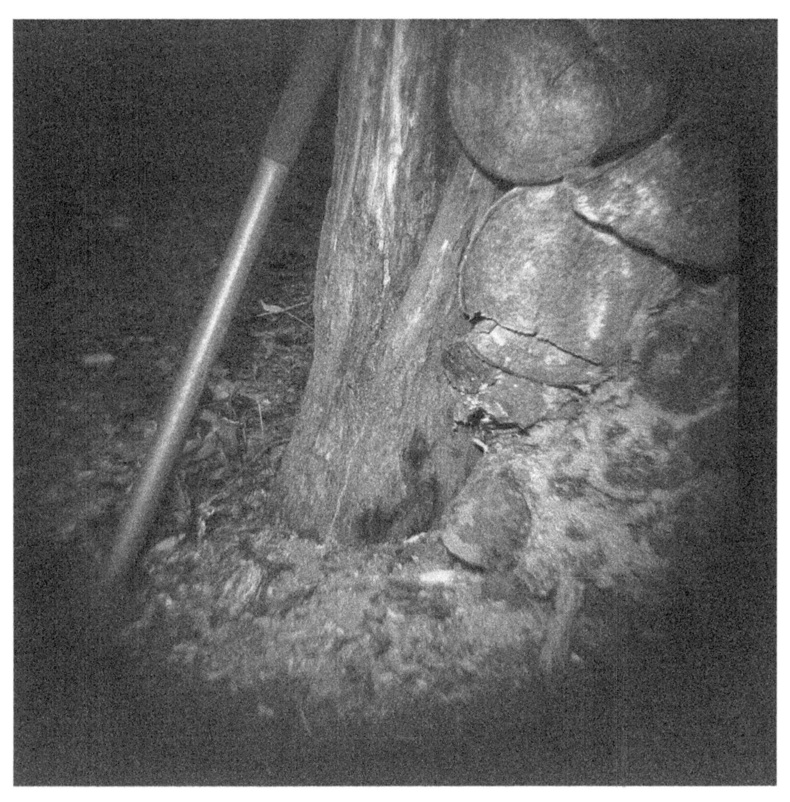

## Dinner Memory

When my mother was young, younger than I am now, and I was a child, she worked at a Hardee's serving burgers through a window. Once a man drove up to the window naked, save for his seat-belt, and said, when he went to pay, "ma'am, I seem to have lost my wallet!" Each woman called another over to gawk at his flaccid penis, giggling like innocent girls with virginal eyes. He apologized and drove away, someone writing down his license plate. The police were called, he was arrested and fined, forced to send a letter of apology to the employees:

"So sorry to up-
Set you. I seemed to have lost
My pants. Best wishes."

I wonder how often she thinks of this man, with his genitals just "laying there." Often, I think of her young face telling me this story over dinner, cringing and laughing as I tried to imagine the strangeness lived by adults.

## Reflection: Black Snake

He's supposed to coil then strike, but instead
stretches out as if to draw a box for long division;
maybe he's the Ouroboros or the Midgard
serpent, trying to wrap himself around the world.
Yet, he neither divides nor protects, he simply
seems to wait as the stick nears — not to strike
but to steer the iridescence of slick black scales off
the dull burnt charcoal colored asphalt: a mission
to save him. But all snakes tie their tongues up in
lies to do the devil's work: they tempt, they hide,
they disguise. And maybe that's why someone
swerved to hit this serpent so that now only half
his body can reach and when pushed with a stick
he doesn't bother to hiss, recoil, swell, or shrink.
Instead he stiffens and waits. A swarm of yellow
jackets attacks his face, he writhes in legless pain,
and one crawls from the mouth while others aim

for the eyes. And two failed saviors stand dumb over this grave: trying desperately to shoo the insects away, yet not strong enough to end the poor black snake.

## Dam Building/Dam Breaking

Your hands cold
Reaching deep
In creek water
To move boulders
For our dam.
Did our movements
Disturb the crawdads?

I'm remembering
Those hands
That water
The weather
Grey sky
Dead leaves
And the shape
Of the creek —
Serpentine.

And later,
Only a day,
I tore down our dam
Because I didn't
Understand the way
One dam
On a little creek
Wouldn't prevent another
From holding water
In autumn.

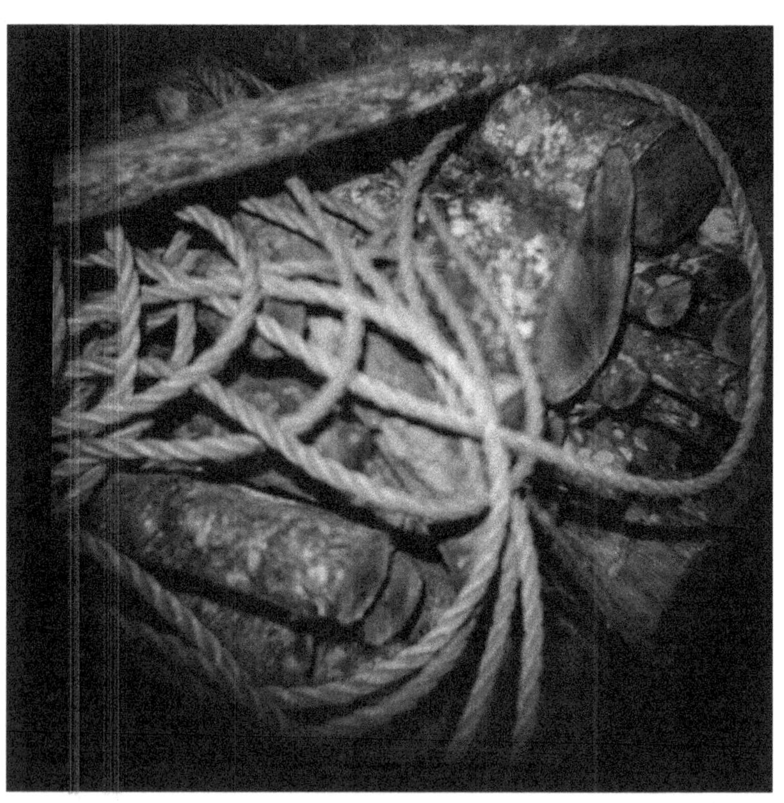

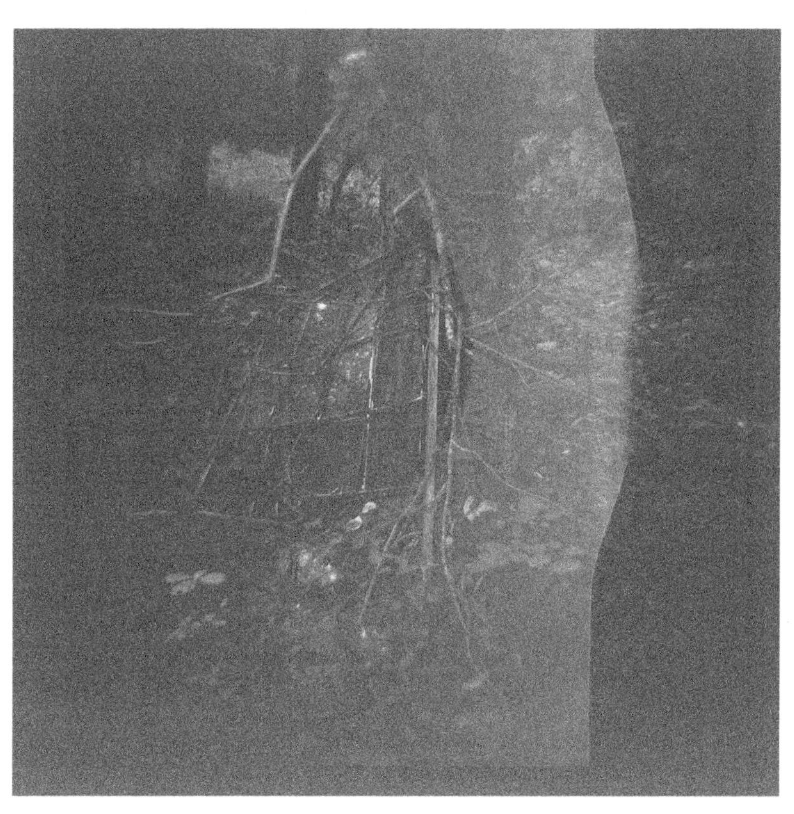

## Reflection: Ghost of a House

Bare mattress springs beneath dead leaves, the fabric long lost to rust, creates treacherous terrain for young feet. Among the wreckage there, broken window frames, rusted coffee cans in frail decay, and little old medicine bottles of cobalt glass — precious treasures with tiny terrariums inside, growing moss where nothing else could reside. So much and yet no walls, no floor, no single bit of shingle to prove this garbage was once a home. Yet, with enough digging, a doll head black with loamy soil appears broken in partial dry rot from the cycle of the years. What little one played here, and was he careful, reckless, or ignored? Maybe the house burned down. Maybe it caved in. Maybe it disappeared without a family to remind it into existence. Maybe it needed someone else's heart to keep its own beating.

## **Rummy Memory**

Mother,

It's summer,
Sandwiches and Cheetos
On Styrofoam plates,
And we are sitting on the floor
Around the living room
Coffee table
Playing games.

I play my two on your twos,
And you play your six on mine,
Then it's rummy on the board
For the second time.

And when I think I'm out of cards
I yell, "I win!"
But you remind me,
One, I'm only floating,
And two, we're playing to five hundred.

**Food Memory**


Father,

How do you make
Fried chicken livers
So well
When you can't even stand the smell
Of them cooking?

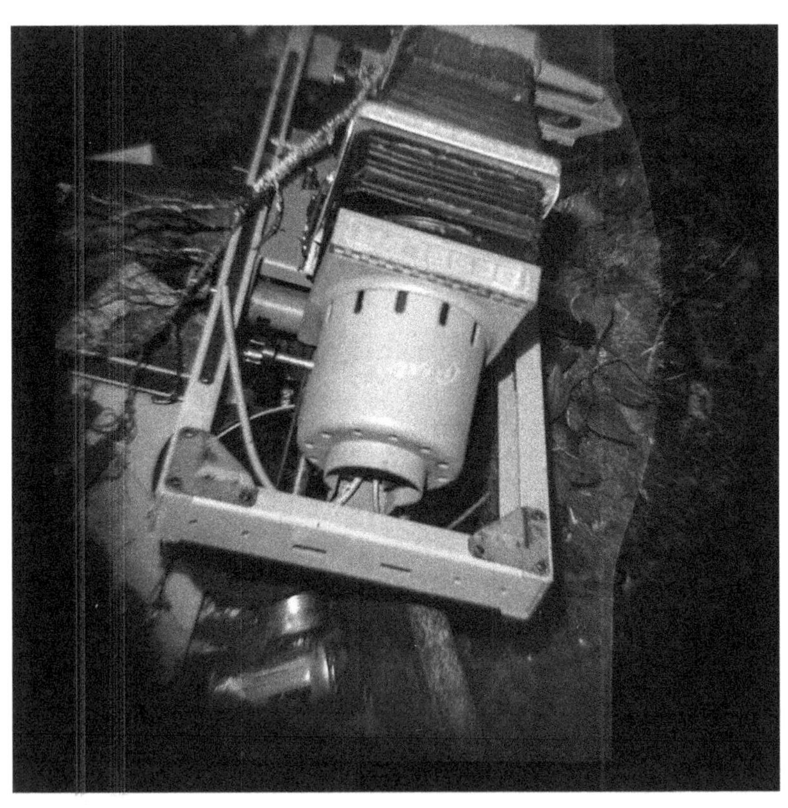

## Imagined Manhoods

I. Stag

Having offered the heart of a stag
To the altar of sky,
He replaces his tie
With bloodied hands.
His wife will find no lipstick collars,
Only sanguineous stains
The size of finger prints
Around each pearlescent button.
She will wonder, yet again,
Why men must hunt naked —
As if her sex were never feral,
As if she never felt the moon!
She will wash what he dirties,
Cook and clean his murders,
But he gets to howl,
Holding bowels above his head.
The husband gets the kiss of sun

At dawn and dusk,

When mosquitoes,

Attracted by his musk,

Get caught and die in his chest hair.


II. Deer


Having worn the pelt of a deer —

Still warm and bloody,

Newly removed and waiting

To be tanned —

He examined the Rorschach tests

Left with religious symmetry

Like portent birthmarks

About his chest.

Each port wine smear,

Each drying patch of life

Shifting red to brown,

Became a mark ancestral:

King and clown
Hunter and hound —
These are the faces
Looking back at him now.
He found what he sought:
The company of wolf and hart.


III. Hart


Having drank from the skull of a hart,
He commended himself
On a job well done,
On making use of every part.
In school he'd read
That Indians wasted nothing,
Tanning hide with brain
Made teeth into tools;
He envied their industry,
Imagined their efficiency

As if it were his own,
Walking alone through the forest.
Now he was a wild man!
He saw himself as tribal!
He was in touch with the Great
And the Spirit of that Greatness!
Sipping homemade mead by the fire,
He thought, "I'm free!
A man who remembered
How to use what he kills."

## Rural Route 4, Box 358 II

A labyrinth of serpentine dirt roads, as if M.C. Escher turned a circle inside out and found a den of snakes slithering: I grew up among such curves, dusty and crying out for rain. But one foot away, forests lush with decay — the smell of peat and loam and ferns and moss. A wood in bloom, grown on a bed of loss, the way all beauty grows from dross. My father swung me through the contours of those whorls, in his truck through the arches of parabolas. Trees tight against the cab — amazing that we never lost a mirror through these runs.

**Klan Encounters Pt. 2**

There are still hoods,
And they pass their pamphlets out
Outside Ingles
And Food Lion
As if they nourish
With their hate.

They have, too
Stood outside the entrances
Of my schools
And handed their literature
Up and in
Through the bus windows,
As if they offered
An education
With their hate.

## Reflection: In the Distance

Grey dust clings to the once green greenery, mostly weeds and saplings, lining the edges of the dirt road. Each small plant in its own crematorium of stirred-up holocaustic decay. Can they breathe below that layer of rock dust? Do they long for rain, when with every passing car the dust deepens and distances a dream? And in the background, like a painting, is nature pristine despite the foreground of travelers and the trash they've heaved from moving windows of camping cars or adolescent nights drinking: aluminum cans marked with the insignia of beer and cola, blue or red, patriotic consumerism on the frontier; candy wrappers; fast food bags — now made eco-friendly in brown to show off the ability to biodegrade… all evidence that man buries what he loves when near in order to see a more perfect version far away.

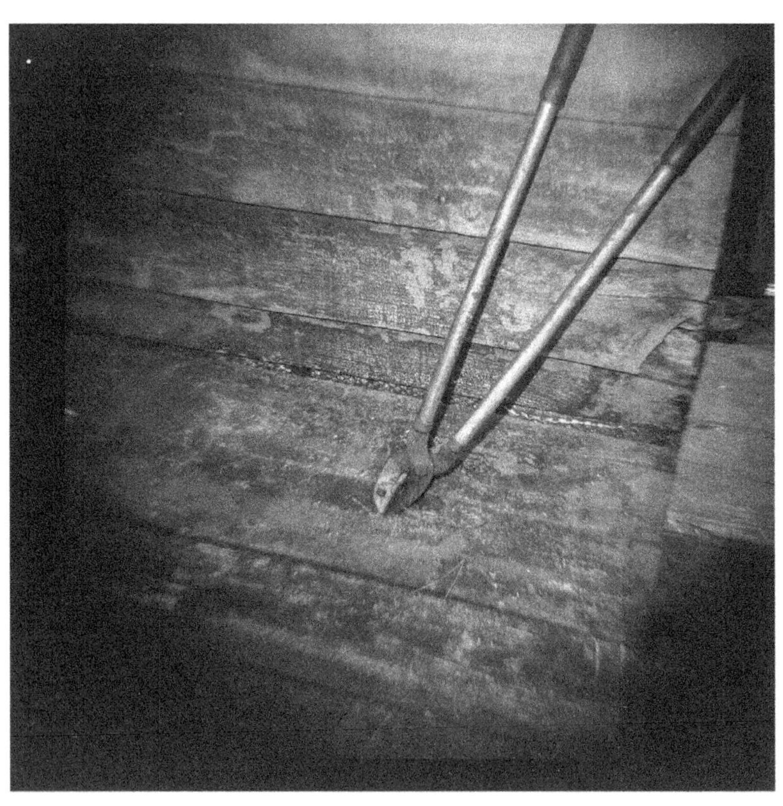

## Memory in Tritina

Father,

Do you remember walking me through the
    woods,
Showing me the big swing and the tree house
    you built,
The old logging roads you used to hike in youth?

I remember the path we took, a shared
    landscape of youth:
The umbrage, foliage, bent trees, sign posts of
    the woods.
Had we taken more days like this, what would
    we have built?

But to be fair, I was never able to construct, to
    build,
True both in my adulthood and in my youth…
It wouldn't have mattered if we'd spent more
    time in the woods.

Remember my youth and the trails we built in
    the woods.

## Memory Recipe

No. 1

Sweet tea was easy, and maybe because of that, it was the first thing you taught me. Three bags, family sized, loaded into the filter. Then fill the reservoir with water, turn it on and wait.

Meanwhile, put two cups of sugar into the gallon picture. If you're on a diet, a cup and a half will do, maybe even a cup and a quarter. Then when the percolator has completed its brew, let steep, then add it to the sugar and make a simple syrup. Finish with cold water. Refrigerate and serve with ice.

No. 2

Lasagna, you taught me, requires browning of the meat, a little spice — salt, pepper, a sprinkle of Italian blend; then simmer with your favorite red sauce from a can. You can drain the grease or leave it — it's a matter of taste, and richness. In the background, the noodles should be boiling this whole time.

We start with sauce, you said. A thin layer on the bottom of the Pyrex pan; then a layer of noodles, long ways, followed by ricotta, followed by sauce, then noodles again — this time short ways across rather than up and down. You said it made it more stable, better able to stand up.

Repeat these steps: sauce, noodle, cheese until we reach the edge, then cover the top with mozzarella, and bake. 350 degrees for an hour or until it's browned and bubbling. Everything already being cooked, it didn't matter how long it was in or how warm the oven — just that there was burnt cheese and oozing edges.

And then we'd eat it, always too soon, with the center like napalm dripping down our chins even after blowing on our forks. The recipe said to wait twenty minutes, to let it stand, solidify — but clearly, that was not a rule we followed.

No. 3

Any dinner needs a recipe, even if it's as simple as
the instruction for setting the table: one plate for
each place setting, a fork and knife, a glass with
ice, and pot holders on the table — this is a trivet
free house — to block heat from the skillet.

We serve ourselves. Pass around garlic bread and
talk and eat.

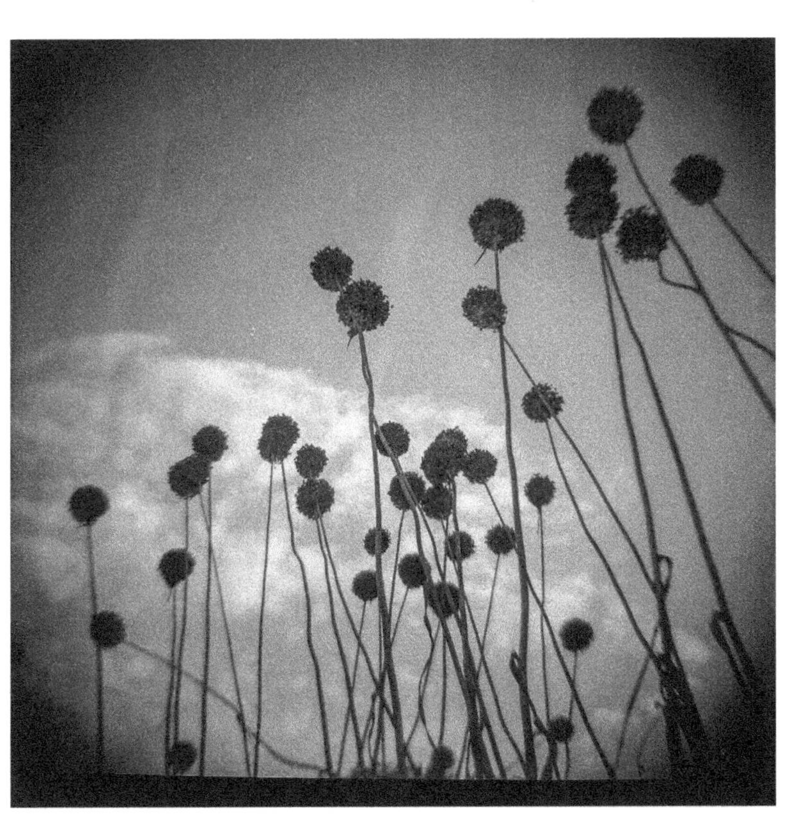

## Reflection: Kudzu

Below the quivering leaves sits an old wood skeleton fused with roots. Vines like veins invade the limbs that hold a sheet metal roof with resolve, acting as Atlas. Reach between the strands, part them, and slip inside. The sun shines through like a green cathedral — stained-glass and gold-leafed lead; but everything inside is dead, and what remains gives up the story of a barn left in neglect. Turn the troughs over and make pews. Collect the rusted tools and build a shrine to this carpetbagger vine, this southern style disease of botany, this creeping floral lush of parasitic climb. If in this church there were a sermon, it'd be of half-truths and half-lies told by old men in an assertive but speculative style:

"Its only enemy is the goat! A goat eats faster than the damn stuff grows!" "Y'know with good rain and the sun, that shit can grow a foot or more a day!" "You can't even burn it! The roots go too deep!" "That shit is Japanese! They brought it in to fight erosion and it took over!"

It took over homes and sheds and fields and trees, it creeps up and slowly suffocates things. Yet it's vibrant, alive, and coats decay like a blanket, covering rot and making beautiful abstract shapes:

"Those ones look like people dancing!" "And them too, only she is falling." "That one there is all alone, kneeling like The Thinker, a saint on the field of kudzu." "Yeah! This one looks like a bone."

Back below, beneath the roof that is coated with leaves, take solace in the silence, the decay, the meditative space, look through the curtain of shimmering green — look for what hides inside, what hides beneath. Look for the space between erosion and growth so rapid it becomes a cancer. Or maybe, just look for quiet and shade.

## Remembering

Sometimes, mother, you
Ask me to remember things —
Beautiful things we shared.

You may tell me,
When a conversation goes quiet
Or when I'm angry, to remember:

The dragon flies collected themselves
Around flowers frequently called weeds,
And buzzed an atonal symphony on their wings.
Green shimmered, as well as purple,
The two opposing pigments
Somehow blending into black against the setting sun —
Each one reflecting in the other,
Until they meld
Making an ineffable color —
Something only nature could create
In a baking summer evening
Along a dirt road,
In a half-circle field.
Slender long bodies of metallic magic
Weaving between briar and broken limb…
What is there to forget?

## Reflection: Last Times

Everything is dying at different speeds. So much is seen for the last time, as if leaving home was a way of life for runaway eyes, as if there were no other forces acting upon bodies in motion — but alas, decay equally corrodes, hides, reveals, and obfuscates. A feather falls from the sun, drifting in circles of blue/black silence. Branches break just inside earshot. A corpse loses its skin to insects and the elements. Rain. Thoughts move in waves just the same, tides rising over footprints to strip them away: Will this face smile again? Will these papery hands hold close together familiar fingers? Will the plow rust or change the landscape? Either way, the creaking of the roof proves that it is going to give, even if not today; everything else is just the same.

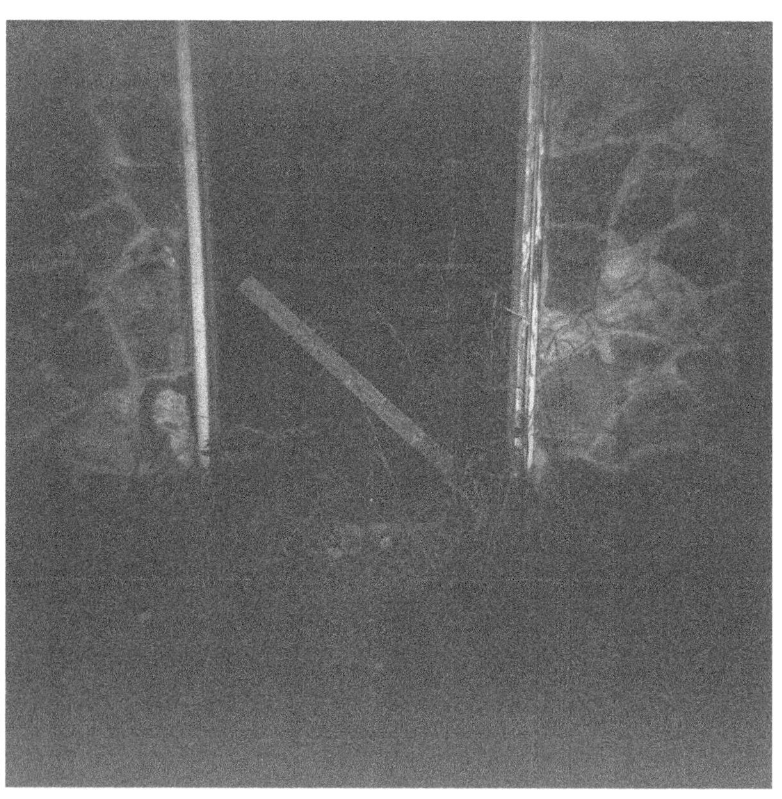

# Listening Memory, or Childhood Guilt

Silent children hear secrets.
I hear my mother speaking
As I pretend to sleep —
My door open just enough
That the light peaks in
beams across my floor.

The light starts narrow and
Then spreads wide — just like
My mind when it hears the words.
I can't believe the light
That pierces the darkness — ever
Widening as my mind processed.

Her world has not been beautiful.
And for that she cries real tears
About the hurt of my father and hers.
I hear her scream to her sister
About the distance between them —
Honesty that can't be unheard.

I want to give up the details,
To repeat every phrase, and
For what I can't remember well,
Just make up something to tell.
But those are not my stories,
Even if I overhear them…

Even if I shouldn't eavesdrop,
Even if I could plug my ears,
Even if I should close my door,
I don't do what I should —
I don't comfort her,
I only listen as she speaks.

## Rose Memory

Father,

You covered the sheer bank
Beside the house
With a sprawling vine
Of climbing roses.
Another one
You planted
In the backyard
With a special lattice fence
To facilitate its growth.
Was it just me,
Or did you think
Every bare space
Deserved beauty?

## Rural Route 4, Box 358 III

A division, marked at first by a single sign: Dead End. Later came Hidden Drive, then Greenfield Ln, then simply Stop; and when the pavement came, so did Pavement Ends, then Single Lane. They read less as a warning, and more a note on the uselessness of taking that course, suggesting the unworthiness of the tread that would be lost against the gravel en route. The signs were not for those who lived among them, but for the interlopers looking for leaves and apple orchards. Such signs, a division, a marker of who knew the way and those looking, gazing.

## Klan Encounters Pt. 3

There are still hoods,
White and pointed,
Ghostly silhouettes
That gather round
The town square
For a yearly rally
To raise the spirits
Of Southern hate.

It's black magic
In white robes
With little red crosses
On the arms
And a bullhorn
Firmly palmed.

They work adeptly
And ruffle both sides
With their talk:
"Gays and coloreds
Taking over" as
They move in.

As a child we'd drive through
To get a look at them:
At the Klansmen
On the courthouse steps,
At the state police
On rooftops with rifles,
And the protestors
From Atlanta and maybe even
Further out of town.

A spectacle made
Of glittering rage —
Both sides vying
For a stage.

## Reflection: Rocking Chair

Something here is loose. There's a rattle. A squeak. Maybe the wood is settling its match with the weather and decided on swell or shrink. But there's a creaking, not just in the back and forth swing on the arched chair feet, but in the butterfly that isn't landing on the Black Eyed Susans, and in the rain cloud that hangs in space like a menacing moon. Is it in the floor? The foundation? The decorative spines that make up the back — each one carved just so, one delicately shaved wooden ball atop another? Listen to the groaning of the pines; brother tree calls out to brother plank. Maybe each mourns the other. Maybe old ghosts inhabit old porches; maybe they sit side-by-side in still rocking chairs and loosen the bolts, rattle the screws, and massage the wood till all the creaks and groans are gone.

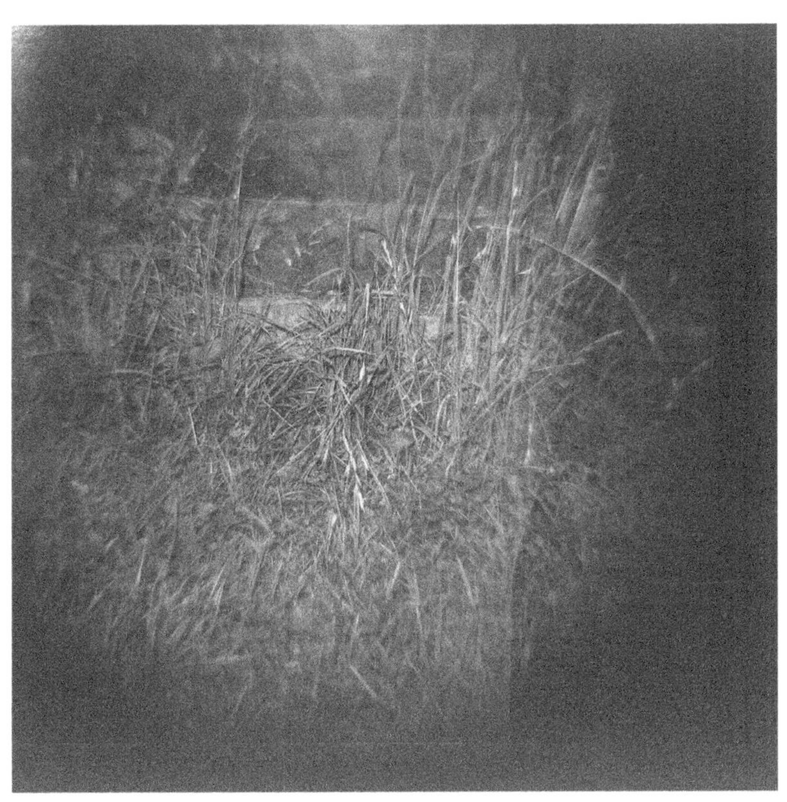

## Hair Memories

I.


Mother,
Dyeing her hair,
And me,
Helping her wash it out in the sink.

II.


The first grey hair
Her father pulls from her head.
The first grey hair
I tell her not to pull.

III.

In a photograph it reaches,
One long black arm,
Down past her hips.
A vague memory
Shows me reaching up for it.

IV.

A cup of water collected
And set with precision
On the brown carpet floor.
I dip the comb
Before running it through her hair —
Amazed at how the wetness
Lets the teeth glide,
Making her hair into silk.

V.

Cut into a bob, once,
I replaced all those memories
With the hair she has now —
As if the present
Changes the past.

VI.

Once or twice
She and I
Did hot oil treatments together.

VII.

My hair was always
Too greasy,
But hers was just right.

VIII.


At times it floated like feathers
Abandoned by birds
Who, in flight,
Were overwhelmed by the wind.


IX.


Other times it was a satin pillow.


X.


And still other times
It was satin on her pillow.

XI.

As a little boy
Sleeping in bed with his mother,
I would pet her hair
Flat against the cushion.
And as a baby,
I'm told,
I'd hold it tight
In my fists
As she held me in the cradle
Of her arm.

XII.

I remember the smell of her perms,
Both when she'd put them in for curl
And when she'd put them in
To tame the waves.

XIII.

Before I was born,
She dyed it black like a crow.
I only know from one picture,
But in it,
The sides fly back like a bird —
Wings taking flight.
Leaving the earth.

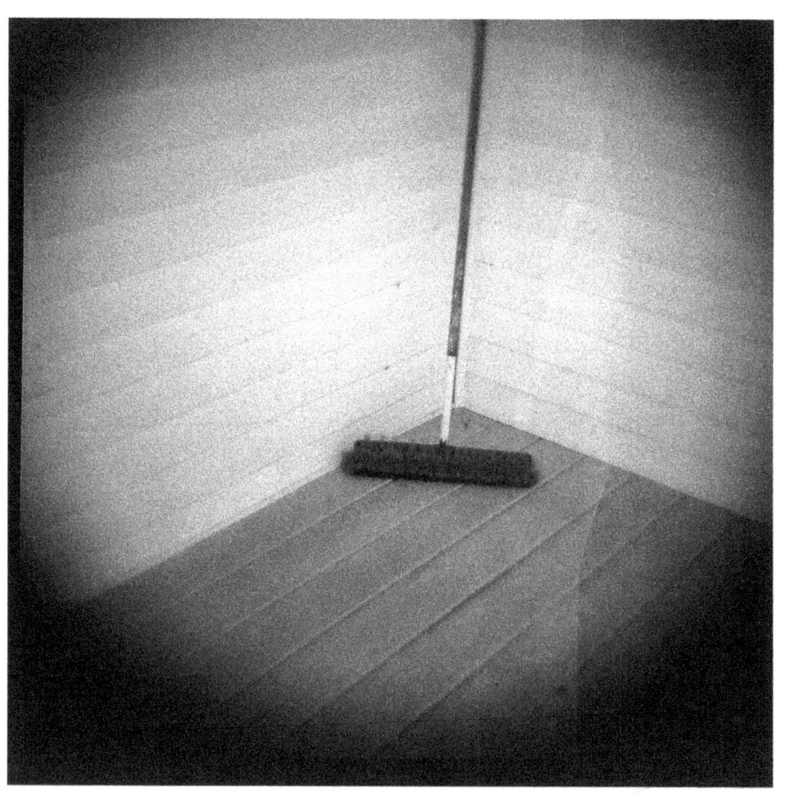

## Bottles

Do you remember the bottles we collected by the creek and the old ruins of the still where we tromped like wild things in the forest?

Do you remember how the bottles held those little worlds inside, the ones that grew moss and ferns and how we'd watch the rain within them drizzle down as if lightning could occur at any moment?

Do you remember how, like them, youth too is a microcosm, just without the glass? Or maybe, possibly, a different kind.

Do you remember the bottle tree we made off the old logging road with the containers that didn't hold a moldy home, or how we filled each empty jar with little bits of water so that we could play them, clinking — our own glass instrument?

Each, a piece in my menagerie of adolescent wanderings in weeds and old logging roads.

## Pontiac Firebird

I remember you, my mother,
Black eyed and crying,
Delivered from the ineffable violence
Of a car crash.
This, the time when
"Some idiot ran [you] off the road"
Into the bottomless hole
Off the blacktop
That reached from peak to peak
Along the mount road.
You, on your way to pick me up
From my grandmother's house.
I was five or six but not seven;
Just old enough
To understand
Both fault and luck,
And I knew that somehow
I sent you into that hole:
Your blue-black firebird

Crumpled from impact.
I never asked how you got out,
But for this one instance
I choose to believe angels
Lifted you from the wreckage —
Bringing you to your mother,
And my mother to me.

## Reflection: Spring House

Daytime darkness, the sun slipping between the slatted wood and beams, landing like snakes of strange blue light that swam among the tranquil waters, showing there the slightest ripple in its slither. A strange magic possessed the space, along with cobwebs and unseen nests for squirrels and birds and feral things; this magic — the merging of building and land — suggesting somehow it is possible to contain the wildness of a river, and bring the power of its coolness to the tasks of civilized man. To think that long ago, some family, name and history unknown, chilled their summer fresh melons in the shade of this strange water shed, and later sat and watched bats swoop down at dusk to harvest the lightning bugs.

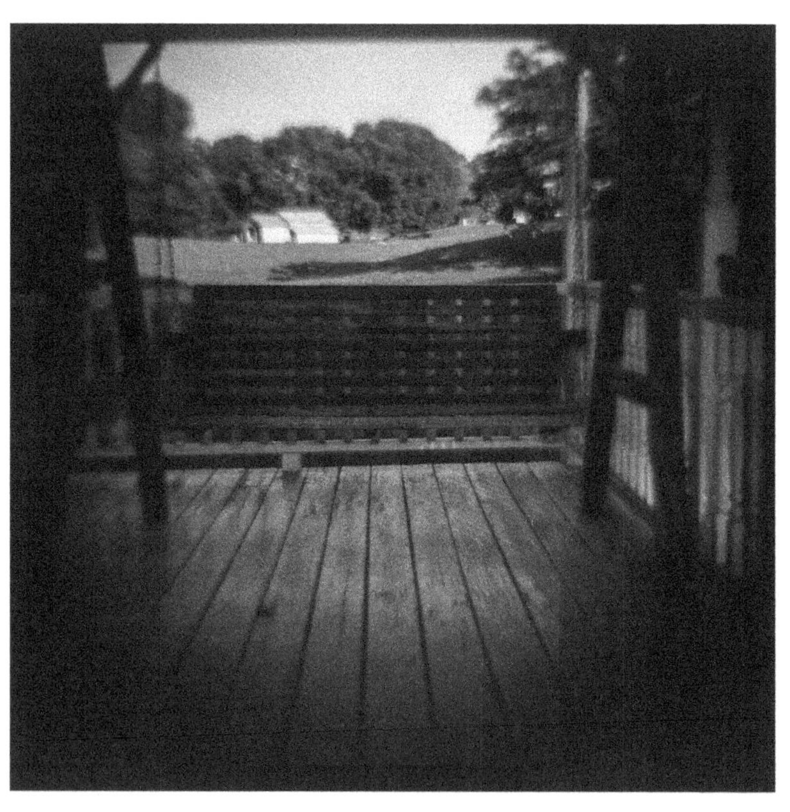

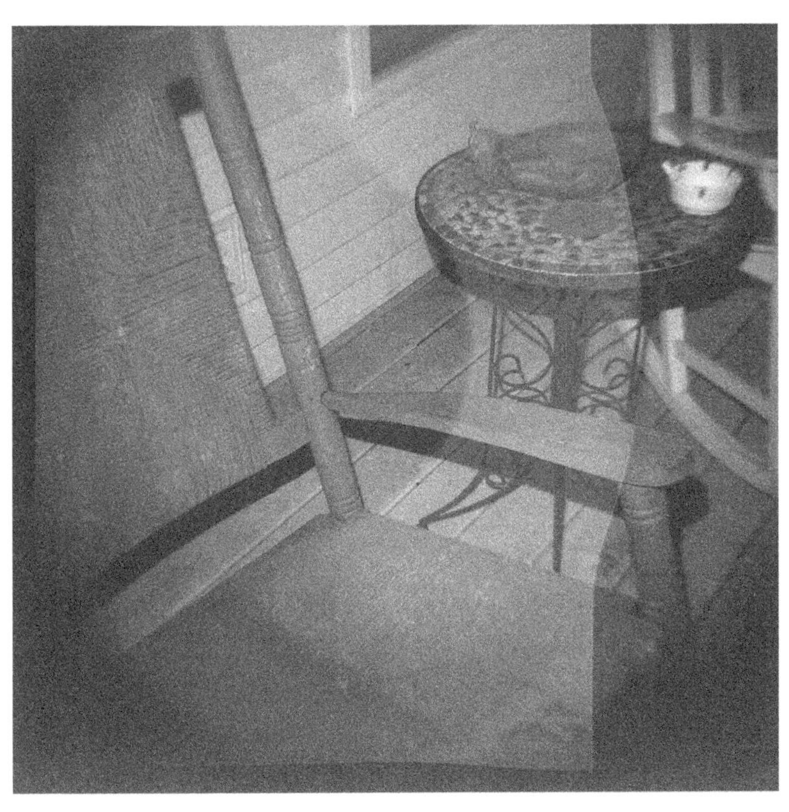

## Rural Route 4, Box 358 IV

A deer in the headlights, every time, gave us pause and the urge to break, sitting silently in the car, never growing tired of the majesty of a buck — counting points in shadows and light — or else a doe, maybe with her fawns — babies still with spots in their coats. There is no number for such stops, for the times we made imaginary windshield eye contact with the fauna of the forest. These stags, these harts, these mammals of glorious brute creation, snorting out fog in winter, locking horns in rut, we saw them and we hoped, maybe, they saw us.

## Father's Shop Memory

There is, tickling the nose of my memory, the smell of sawdust and lumber and rust — all of which I saw resting on the concrete floor and wooded shelves of your shop. There too were wet tools and dissolving blades and things hidden in the backs of other things — that is, things unseen but felt and known. This is the mystery of any father's shop or shed, but this one was yours and by proxy, mine. It was damp always; no water kept out, so mold smell grew in the pine dust too. Here is where you cut the wood, crafted our furniture, applied the stain. This is where you made the world around us.

## Klan Encounters Pt. 4

There are still hoods,
And there are still fires,
Like the gay bed
And breakfast that burned
To the ground
Only a few weeks
After a rally that condemned
Queer residents
And interloping business owners.

Nothing proven.
Nothing disproven.
Just ash to ash
And dust on the breeze.

## Reflection: Strip Mining

Strip malls in the mountains, a new kind of strip mine: just remove the useless soil and trees, plow out a spot for cars to park and wait for business to roll in. But no; each little office sits empty with the ghosts of hope that consumerism would prevail. Instead there's a ghost town among the pines and peaks, some sort of kudzu tumbleweed blows past the marshal's corpse, cobwebs in every corner, gas prices still set to 1998. And then another pops up. And another. Another. John Prine cries for paradise lost, while Joni Mitchell passes out coupons for the Tree Museum — but no one walks by. Everyone's at Wal-Mart if you want to say hi!

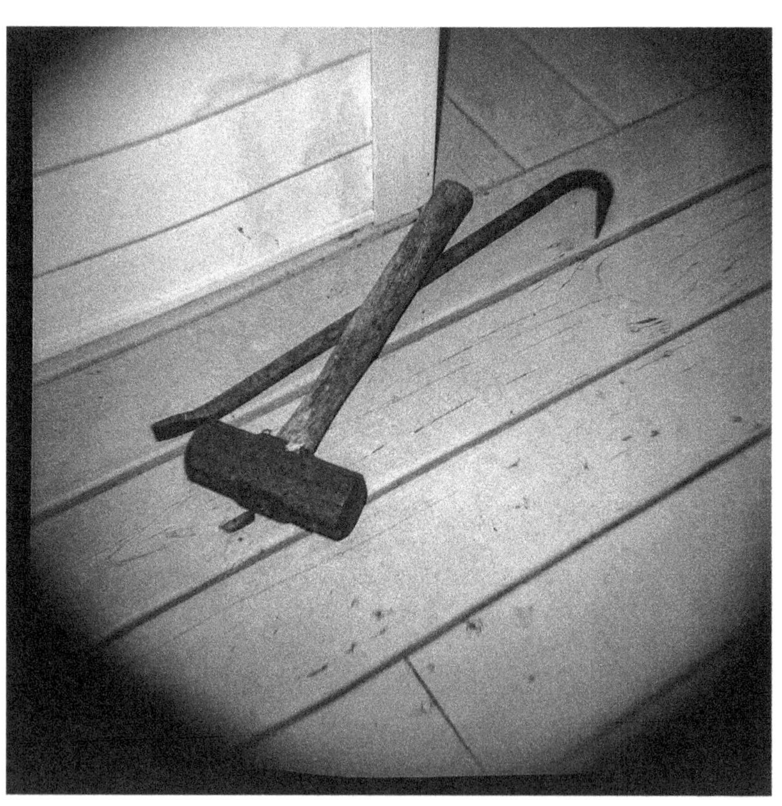

## Watch for Snakes


The butter bowl is filling
With blackberries…

And she is telling me
To watch for snakes
And briars
And chigger-bugs,
But I pay no attention,
Tromping the way
Boys are supposed to trample
Over undergrowth —
Lack of concern,
A sign of masculinity
Poised to blossom.

The butter bowl is filling
With blackberries…

And my bare legs,
Inadequately protected
By my cutoff jeans
And flip-flops,
Are gnawed to nothing —
Just bloody stubs, with
Mosquitoes drawn to the
Moist red cuts.

The butter bowl is filling
With blackberries…

The dogs circle us,
Mixing play with protection
As they mark a parameter
With their doggy piss,
And go patrolling
In overlapping shifts,
Where always one
Stayed by our feet
And the other two
Chase and lose and
Chase and win.

The butter bowl is filling
With blackberries…

And we try to feed them —
The dogs —
Fox grapes and berries,
Thick skinned muscadines,
Both the green and purple kinds.
But they spit them all out
As we laugh
At the lapping of air
Made by their mouths
To save themselves from the
Tart astringency.

The butter bowl is filling
With blackberries…

And at one point
We tug the wrong vine,
One attached to a thicket of weeds
And one that hides
A collection of birds —
Were they starlings or snipes?
Wrens or finches?
I'm not sure what season
Each bird is out for…
But when we pulled,
Rattling loose our fruit,
They exploded in a flourish:
A volcano of feathers
Of beaks
And of talons.
Nothing but the sound of wings,
And our startled screams.

The butter bowl is filling
With blackberries…

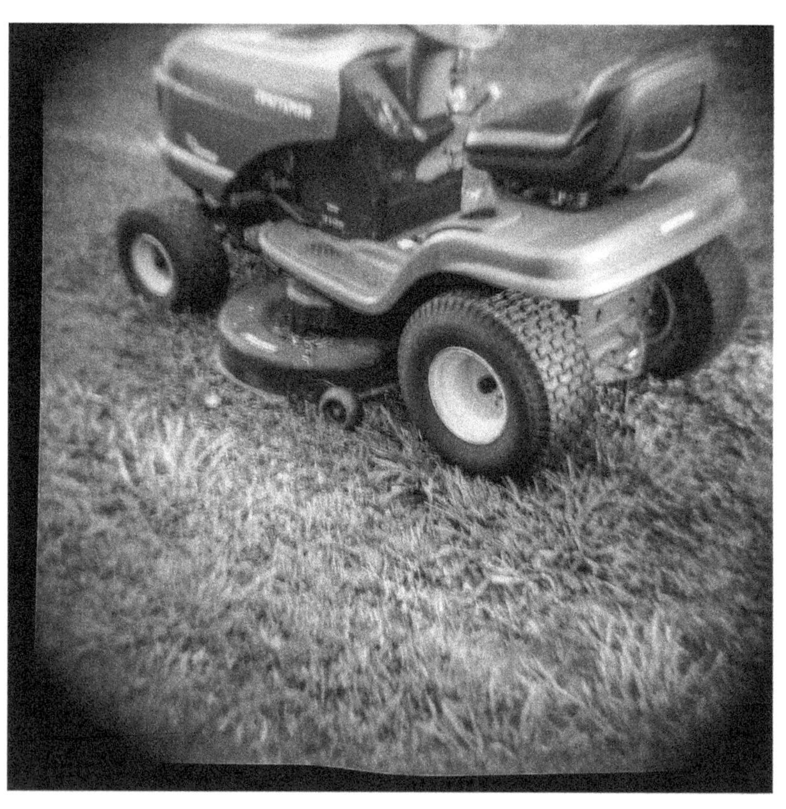

**Reflection: Sunday Mornings**

More churches than could possibly be populated by people each Sunday, each with witty signs outside to advertise revival or salvation or vacation bible school. And even on the busiest of holy days, there have to be more bodies in the graves than pews; I know because the parking lots are often overrun by emptiness, and stray cats in street lights chasing darkness or night bugs. But for those that drag themselves to face the sun, to tie their ties, and primp their smiles on this, the last day of rest, those walls contain life and stories, meaning and family, questions, more questions, and answers they dare not test. Yet, I wish I could see inside the hearts of those that pray, see fully there the illusion that they work so hard to not let shake. But it's mostly wood siding, stained glass, and rose-colored carpet for me; or maybe a story:

"That's the one where my parents got married. Here's the one where my grandfather's buried. I went there once and they spoke in tongues. When I was in middle school this is where we bought drugs."

And if not that I think of the altar calls where children, six and eight and ten, went crawling to get saved; and if not that, I think of that day I begged God to make me feel what it is they say is real, but instead felt the cold emptiness of making my own meaning rather than taking what's been given.

## Nocturna

In the headlights of my driving we saw
The body and the wings of a fairy —
Some magic vision against natural law.
I braked for her and caught her in my light,
A green and purple creature, light and airy —
Proof! Evidence of what lives in the night!
Confirmation of the supernatural
Hanging in the dark among blackberries:
An image burned into our minds — archival.

## Reflection: Time

Pollen season has passed. The wood is stacked. Trash burns in the pit. It smolders, black smoke rising from the tires tossed on top. In the distance, the sound of a creek. Dusk. Crickets and cicada sing. The night birds are quiet. Mosquitoes bite. A porch light comes on. A porch swing creaks at the addition of weight. Soon, a thunderous rain, trees on the line, and no power — just flashlights and the moon. A lit kerosene lamp pulls in the moths. The air is damp with waiting. Change/ unchanging.

## Gardening Memory

I.


When you talk about the old garden,
The long rectangle in the lower yard,
The green forest of vegetation that,
As a natural-explorer-type-kid,
I was swallowed and enraptured
In the density of sky-bound corn…

When you talk about the old garden,
You talk about the way I moved,
Happily and freely between the rows
As you worked diligently in the heat
Of the summer sun, removing weeds.

When you talk about the old garden,
You talk about the bell peppers —
That green dangling fruit, so waxy —
And the way I'd pick them to eat,
Right then! Right off the vine… the
Only time as a child I wanted vegetables.

II.

But I remember other gardens, too.
Times when deer and dogs trampled
Our plants and ate the blossoms off.
I remember the potatoes we planted
In towering stacks of old tires, and
Times they grew, times they didn't,
And the times you were too tired
To care for the garden, to reap or sow
So we all just let it grow over,
Become lawn, returning to not nature.

III.


And then you had the garden moved,
From the lower yard to the back,
Where you put up a protective fence,
Made the whole thing smaller,
Planting only what you'd eat:
Tomatoes, peppers and cucumbers.

Years when you gardened this way,
When there was plenty of rain
And the soil was rich and fertile,
You made salsa and gave it to friends
And family but I ate the most
On thick salty tortilla chips
Or dumping a whole can in my chili.

Every time you made the salsa

It came out different: heat and spice,
Different amounts of tartness.
One year it was sweet with no reason,
Another year it scorched our tongues
And we blamed the temperature
On the jalapeños that composted
In the garden over winter and spring.

IV.

Will you plant your garden this year?

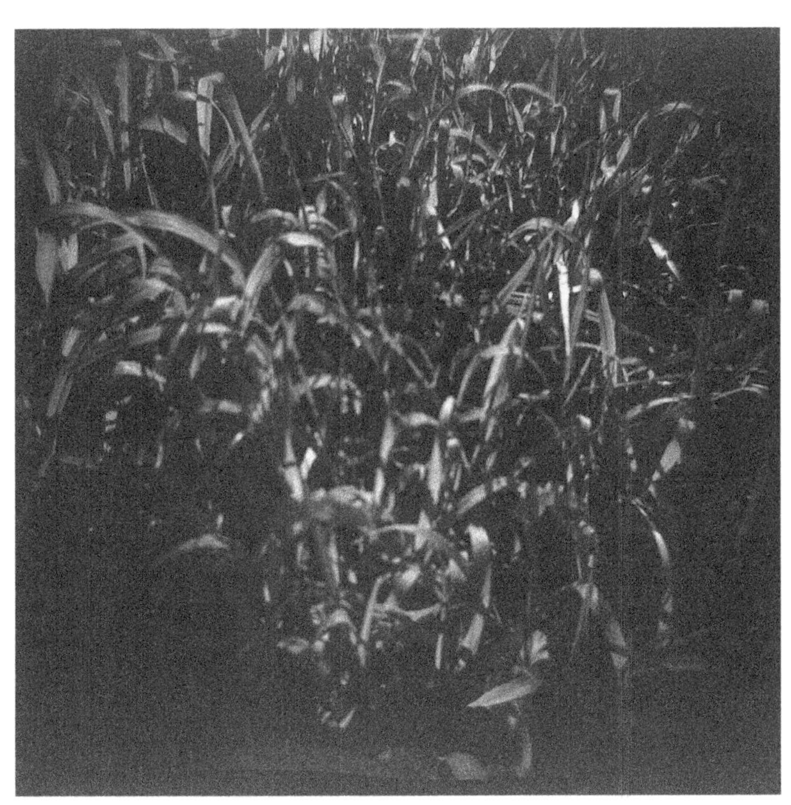

# Angler

One:
we are out on Rainbow Lake,
flat bottom boat and trolling motor.

Two:
fishing off the banks of a river,
you cut your hand on a catfish.

Three:
a dock and tackle box –
I don't remember catching anything.

Four:
getting my first fishing pole,
were we ever closer?

Five:
Carter's Lake, the sky growing grey,
is this a canceled wish?

Six:
another lake,
it started to rain and you found us a tree frog.

Seven:
someone took us on their motor boat —
we fished like kings!

Eight:
remind me.

## Rural Route 4, Box 358 V

Walking barefoot on the dirt and gravel roads, dragging my soles though the cool sandy lulls — I spent a summer checking the mail every day, an excuse for peaking in our neighbor's mailbox to see if he'd gotten a Playboy or some other dirty magazine, which had he ever, I would have stolen, and hid inside my treehouse; the one to which I walked, still with naked soles, through the leaves and sticks and climbed the ladder to survey the yard and the forest beyond. Sometimes I'd rest the pads of my feet in the soothing green of lawn grass, a chance to ease the rawness created by my barefoot wanderings. Sometimes, I'd squish the driveway mud between my toes for fun, then other times I'd step heedlessly in dog shit then pissed off I'd take the water hose to my toes before walking inside to feel the soft carpet.

## Klan Encounters Pt. 5

There are still hoods,
Some of them removed,
Taken off in shame
Or apology.
Some of them young
With sorrowful eyes
Seeking sympathy.

There was a plea
In the newspaper
After a rally
For community forgiveness
From a sixteen-year-old boy
Who helped organize
And advertise
And recruit.

My family knew him,
My parent's friends of his parents,
I'd been to their house,
I'd eaten their snack cakes
Drank their cold cans of Coke.

And I wondered then,
My seventh-grade year,
How many other Klansmen
I'd known without knowing.

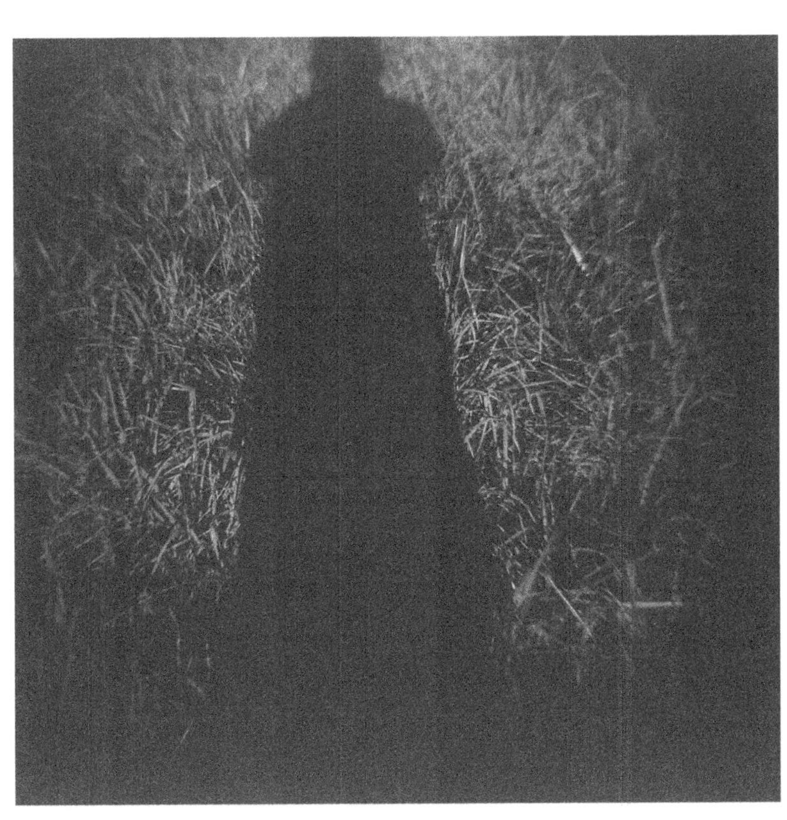

## Reflection: Tools

Every rusty woodshed tool has been collected, and on a line dried sheet, organized in terms of use from oldest to small. These are scepters for the kings of decay; among them are the ax, the awl, the planer, the saw, wire cutters and a set of stately gloves. The condition of each may suggest use or lack thereof, but regardless they wield symbolic power even if lost among the weeds or propped against a porch beam; they both propose questions and demand answers: What family tree did these shears divide? Who was forced to whom with the vice? Did the hammer build or pull apart with claw-like teeth, one nail at a time, from siding, stud, or shingle? The answer is at the bottom of a moonshine jar.

## Mercy Killing

Once you came home nearly crying, your truck
dented — possibly bloody — and told us around
the table that you had hit a deer, not quite killed
it, and had to shoot it to keep it from suffering.

I imagined its face. Having seen a dog die from
being hit by a car, I thought it might be panting
and twitching. But deer don't do more than snort
so it would have made no little yelping sounds.
But it hurt enough you had to kill it. And that
hurt you.

I remembered, too, that when I was six or
seven my grandmother, driving me home from
somewhere, saw a dog hit on the side of the road.
She said, "someone oughta shoot it." I asked why
and she told me sometimes you have to kill things
to save them.

## Alliteration Memory


Saturdays, Sundays, sleeping in…
The soft scent of sizzling eggs,
Bubbling up through butter:
An announcement of comfort coming
In the form of omelets and grits.
How many happy mornings spent like this?
Over my favorite breakfast,
Bringing my eyes to the brightness of the day.

Did I ever say thank you?

## Reflection: Watershed

Funny how the creeks take shape: mountain and valley determine much, and what is left they relegate to liquid power, leading all the runoff into waterfalls, narrow passages between rock walls, and pools, great pools, all pools — the large, the deep, the shallow, and the small, collected here for swimming and bathing, quiet reflection of thoughts and leaves in the fall. But with width of field and level ground, the motion carves the shape more than the landscape dictates the flow of water, silt, and rain; here on the foothill fresh alluvial plain, the creek snakes serpentine among the deer that steal hidden bites of corn and crops and grain. In a wide spot, between the banks of clay, a tiny sandy delta divides the water so that youths in play can tromp across, dry and unaware of the forces that have shaped their day.

## Creation Myth

In the beginning, there was darkness, a book, and two bodies coming together on your birthday. God said let there be light and there was light, but you turned out yours for the night — I know because the couple in the book did the same. Like Adam before Eve, like the man in the book before his wife, you and god were lonely and needed a mate. Then, like Adam and Eve, like god and his creations, like the illustrated couple in my book, you were fruitful — you multiplied. This book — "Where Babies Come From" — showed a kiss and then a swirl of magic and mist in purple and grey, the cartoon depiction of romance; and I imaged my creators — you and my father — like the chaos before god separated the heavens from the waters. I knew it was this chaos, your water, and my father's Holy Spirit that made me. I imagine I was born on the sixth day? Did I give order to things? Did I walk around like Adam in the garden with the power to name?

## Reflection: Logging Road

Carved into an earthly layer cake, the once jagged walls of clay and roots have worn smooth into a slope of leaf covered decay. Sapling pines spring from the muck in hopes of growing tall to reach the sun — but there is far to go. Just ask the senior trees, those that rose up from the barren hills to rebuild, rebuild, rebuild a world of dirt to evergreen. And with every passing day another ring wraps around those conifers — both elder and sapling — and the needles and the leaves that fall create another layer of geology, a soil sample left to measure time or simply to be scraped away for the next excuse for progress, the next excuse to trim, cut back, and then reseed.

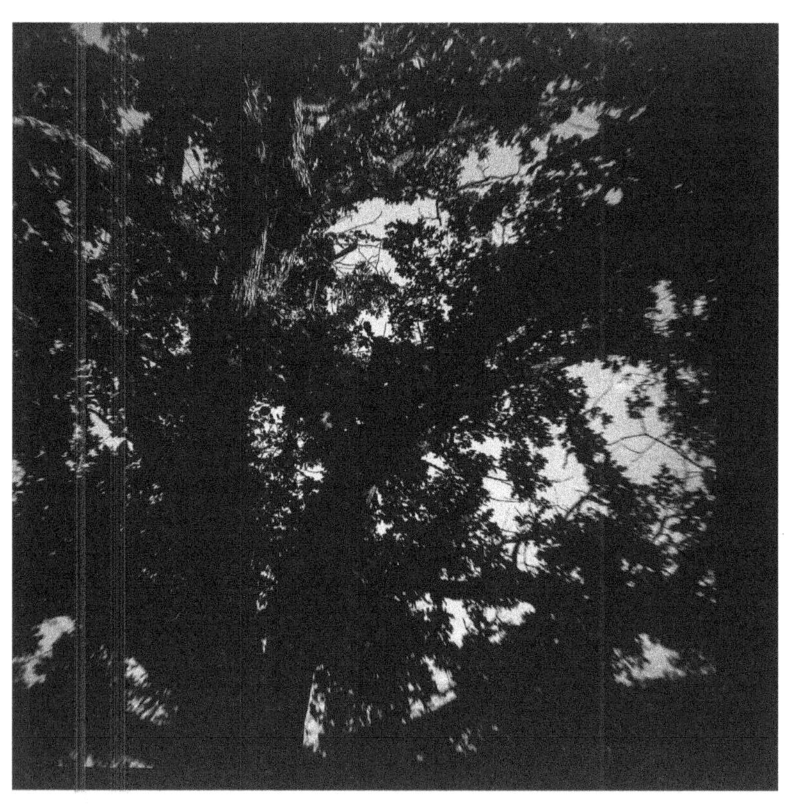

## Poetics of Space

The front door moved at least three times.
Once, coming home, I forgot where it was;
Nearly tripping over the lumber on the porch —
Stumbling safely in the darkness back into
What was to become another living room.

In starting position, the door was by the kitchen,
And we could see out the window from dinner,
Where we gathered around the table when
Arriving guests would trample up the porch stairs,
And wave through the window at us eating.

But then the window was covered over
And the porch enclosed to grow the living room,
Then the door moved over to double the space
For more couches, a bigger TV, and a fireplace…
But we were left without a line of sight outside…

So the door was moved again, four feet over
To clear the path from your seat to the door,
All this to enable you to see who's coming
To interrupt dinner: the mailman or family
Or simply someone lost and turning around.

Did moving the door fix the way
You felt the house was always on the wrong angle,
Putting out its profile and not its smile?
Did moving the door change the space
Enough that you felt like you had a new place?

When I stand and look around me now,
I see all the varied insides of this old house.
I see every moved front door, and all at once.
I see every window removed, added, or replaced.
I see each couch and furniture arrangement.

From one spot I see my leaving in a fit of anger,
I see you leaving but in the throes of hurt,
And daddy storming out to go who knows where.
I see my friends and your friends walking up
Each walking to a different door — a different place.

I see every patch of carpet, at some point,
With a dog laying on it and you beside them,
Or playing with them, as much pet as person.
You are painting their nails in one corner,
And brushing their coats in another.

I see your fingerprints, my mother's fingerprints,
In every nook and on every surface of this house,
The house my family lived in and lives in,
Even without me there, the house persists…
The house you touched; the house my father built.

## The Sound of Home

Home is the sound of hammers hitting nails and making me blink every time — the sound of nails as you added and subtracted and rearranged the house as if it were a puzzle box.

Home is the sound of dogs barking to greet you on your way in the door after work, their "woofs" and "barks" like little "hellos" and "how-are-yous." Later it is the sound of their nails dancing on the linoleum: tic click click tic click click tic.

Home is the sound of your voice saying wake up, then wake up again, then get ready, then get ready again; it's the sound of you saying hurry up or we'll be late.

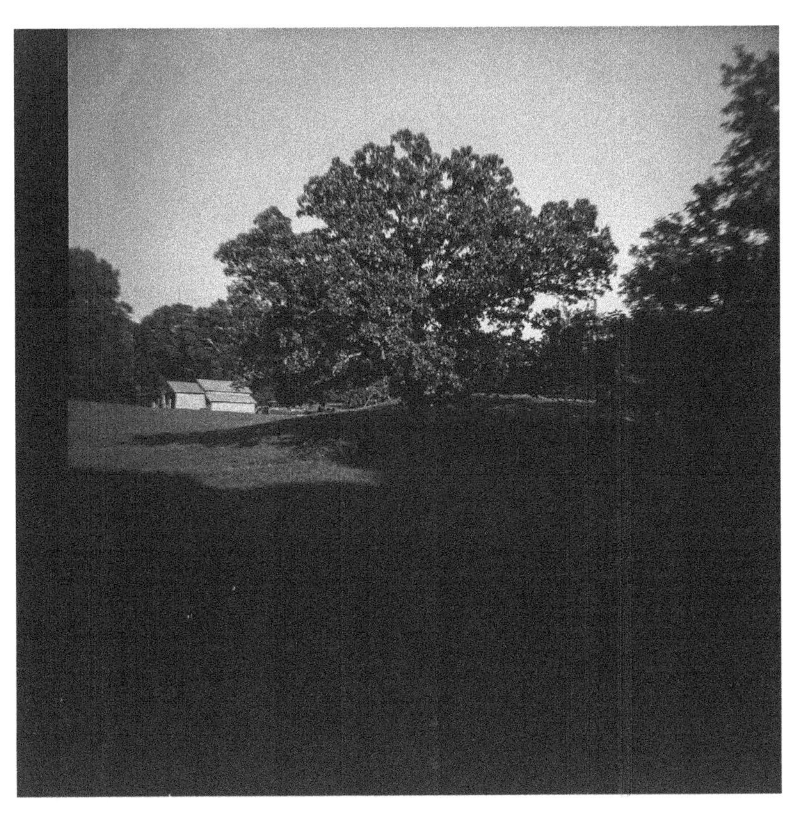

**Carcass Poems**


I. Skink


A lizard loses his tail
To the paw of a cat.
The lizard's loss becomes a snake.
Wriggling. Writhing.
A faceless serpent swimming on land
While my face
Is lost in the dulled varnish of the floor.
I am the stump of the tail.
Heart flickers like tail twitches.
Blinking after the beheading:
I'm counting days
Until cat gut coughs me up
Or brings the severed rest of me
To its owners' door.

II. Chicken

My grandmother,
At a time when I didn't know her,
I'm presuming but am also sure,
Would walk out to a chicken coup
And grab a fathered neck —
Twist.
Cracking like a turtle shell imploding.
A likewise hand is on my neck.
I will become food.
I will be stripped,
Downy white scalded off in boil,
My bones cracked,
My ass stuffed
And my guts gutted…
Death is always,
For someone else,
The beginning of a loving Sunday dinner.

Wringing —
A single spin around a fist —
I won't die fast,
But run headless
Circles in the dirt.
My body missing my beak,
Run ragged and cluckless.

III. Domesticated Dog

Brakes locking wheels.
Unsure where the squeal comes from:
Tires on asphalt or
Rubber on discs.
I know only the thump and the whimper…
A car zooming off.
Old man saying,
"I moved your dog
Out of the road."

A stranger's kindness in death.
I bury myself like that dog,
In leaves that fill the ditch,
Dry symbols of autumn
Persisting into summer —
Crumbling regardless,
Under my weight.
Sheets are the best I have,
All of them,
And a crack between two mattresses;
Your car still in my ears.
Do they have dead dogs in Boston?
A girl, somewhere,
Twenty years ago,
Is screaming in a graveyard.
Black marks mark the black top.
That canine never left the ditch.
Our arms entwine in rot.

IV. Rabbit, and Various Rodents

I feed mice and rats and rabbits
To various sized snakes:
Boas, pythons, even a rattlesnake.
The mice make no noise —
Ready always to accept the nothing.
The rats, sometimes, will bite —
A token marker of their distaste.
But it's the rabbits,
They put up a fight.
And had I not wanted you —
Black snake/iridescent scales —
Suffocating me,
I would push back
With my toe claws,
Bite holes in your tattooed arms…
But I wanted you.
So I thump my foot against the glass of your cage.

I whimper…
(Rabbits piss themselves
When their bodies are released
From life.)
Camouflaged anaconda,
Leave me writhing in my little death…
Swallow me whole.

## Rural Route 4, Box 358 VI

Standing in ditches with butter bowls we fill so full
lids won't fit, cars pass by and people wave in this,
my childhood pastoral. We cannot see their faces
but we recognize their cars, and say, "oh that's the
Wests" or maybe, "that's the family that moved
into old man Johnson's place." But the cars don't
matter so long as they drive slow enough not to
stir up dust and disturb us from gathering ripe
black fruit.

## About the Author

Dudgrick Bevins is an interdisciplinary artist from the North Georgia mountains. He studied English Education, American Studies, and Gender Studies before taking the underground queer railroad north to New York City. He lives with his partner, a fellow artist and writer, and their very grumpy hedgehog, Ezri. He teaches a variety of high school seminar courses and creative writing.

## also by Dudgrick Bevins

*Georgia Dusk* (with luke kurtis)

*My Feelings Are Imaginary People Who Fight For My Attention*


## also published by bd-studios.com

*The Animal Book* by Michael Harren

*Tentative Armor* by Michael Harren

*Angkor Wat* by luke kurtis

*the immeasurable fold* by luke kurtis

*Visions of the Beyond* by Stefanie Masciandaro

*Puertas Españolas* by Josemaria Mejorada & May Gañán

*Here Nor There* by Sam Rosenthal

*Jordan's Journey* by Jordan M. Scoggins

*Just One More* by Jonathan David Smyth

*Retrospective* by Michael Tice